# The **M**useum **O**f **B**ad **A**rt

## Art Too Bad to Be Ignored

Tom Stankowicz and Marie Jackson

A MOBA Publication

Andrews and McMeel
A Universal Press Syndicate Company
Kansas City

*We wish to thank artists Bonnie Daly, Tom McKinley, Aimee Lebec, Sanford A. Winslow, Jeremy Sacco, Frank Oldfield, Sarah Irani, and those whom we have been unable to trace whose work is included in this catalog.*

*Our thanks to Fitzy Huber, Lee McDonald, Susan Lawlor, Donna and Jason Stern, Jim Schulman, Patricia Deardorff, Leigh Weesner, Chuck Furbush, Victor Clark, Garen Daly, Rick O'Hara, and Kathy Sue Levine for finding pieces included in this catalog and donating them to the Museum of Bad Art.*

*Thanks to Alan Ridenour, Richard Gleaves, the Hoffmans, and Gary Hunnicut for allowing us to reprint their letters, and to Ethan Berry, Virtual MOBA Conservator, for his comments on velvet paintings.*

*Grateful appreciation to Tom Baccei, Cheri Smith, and everyone at N E Thing Enterprises, Louise Sacco and Cathi McParland at Backyard Computing, Mark Gregorek and Lisa at Blue Moon, Chris Schillig, Regan Brown and JuJu Johnson at Andrews and McMeel, and our colleagues on the staff of the Museum of Bad Art.*

*A final word of thanks to our families, loved ones and friends and to the Friends of MOBA for their support.*

Stankowicz, Tom.
   The Museum of Bad Art : art too bad to be ignored / by Tom Stankowicz and Marie Jackson.
     p.   cm.
   ISBN 0-8362-2185-0
   1. Museum of Bad Art (Boston, Mass.)—Catalogs.  2. Art—Massachusetts—Boston—Catalogs.  I. Jackson, Marie.  II. Title.
N521.M87S73   1996
708.144'61—dc20
                             96-19444
                                CIP

# Contents

# Contents

## The Institution

Dear Friends,

The Museum of Bad Art is the only institution in the world dedicated to the collection, preservation, exhibition, and celebration of bad art in all its forms and in all its glory. MOBA, as it is affectionately known to its supporters, presented its first public exhibition in April 1994. The response, naturally, was overwhelming.

The pieces in our collection range from the work of talented artists that have gone awry to works of exuberant, although crude, execution by artists barely in control of the brush. What they all have in common is a special quality that sets them apart in one way or another from the merely incompetent.

You have probably asked yourself many times why it is that bad art has, until now, been mysteriously ignored by the cultural institutions of our nation's major cities. Evidence has recently emerged to support our long-held theory that bad art has been silenced by science.

In June 1995, some masterful drawings of beasts were discovered in the French Ardèche region. Scientific analysis has shown them to be at least thirty thousand years old, making them the world's oldest known paintings. It seems they are very good. The oldest previously known cave painting, dated at 27,110 years old, depicts the simple crude outline of a hand. Until the discovery of the Ardèche caves, experts assumed that early drawing and painting began with clumsy lines and only became more sophisticated over centuries. "This comes as a shock to many of us," said Jean Clottess, the French specialist who led the expedition to the paintings. "This shows us that early art, just like art of the past few thousand years, had ups and downs . . . and that there were artists who were more backward or more gifted."

At the Museum of Bad Art we are grateful to M. Clottess for lifting the lid on the conspiracy of silence, disclosing to the world at large for the first time what we have always known. Bad art has been with us from the beginning.

While it is painful to reflect on the countless pieces that have been destroyed in the thirty thousand years preceding the founding of MOBA, this pain seals our determination to find new and more creative ways to bring the worst of such works as remain on our planet to the widest of audiences.

It is with great joy that we introduce this catalog, bringing you a selection of works from our permanent collection. We are confident that it will bring you many hours of pleasure.

Our Acquisition Department is, of course, delighted, since this will no doubt lead to new donations from around the globe. Though the Boston area has been a rich mine for bad art, we have no doubt that every country and every culture has an equally rich bounty waiting to be discovered.

At the back of this catalog you will find information on the important behind-the-scenes work of the Museum of Bad Art, details of our public events program, educational outreach efforts, and answers to many of your questions about MOBA. Most importantly, this section provides the tools you need to do your part to prevent further wanton destruction of our international heritage.

I refer particularly to the submission procedures detailed on page 98, and I urge you to support us in carrying out our important work by joining the Friends of MOBA. An application form is included on page 101. Please share this opportunity with others and avoid mutilating this catalog by photocopying the application form. Many friends of MOBA routinely tuck a copy of this form into each piece of mail they send. We applaud their initiative and invite you to use your creative spirit to spread the news of MOBA like a raging virus, no, like flowers in a spring meadow, across our lands.

Sincerely,

Jerry Reilly
Executive Director

Dear Reader,

As the esteemed curator of the Museum of Bad Art, I am often asked "What makes a painting bad?" or "Just what is Bad Art?" Sometimes the questions come from members of the public who wish to unload gifts of art they have received. At other times the queries are from artists, hopeful or fearful that their work may end up in our permanent collection. These questions are most often put to me by people who have not yet seen the cherished works of MOBA.

The response that remains closest to my heart and nearest to the truth is "I know it when I see it." Visitors to our galleries need look no further than the walls that surround them to get the picture about museum-quality bad art.

The most common error is made by those who equate bad art with bad taste. The famous dogs playing poker and the ubiquitous velvet Elvis paintings have no place in our collection.

*Sunday on the Pot with George* is a large pointillist work that frequently confounds the novice. Clearly, the artist responsible for *George* had complete control, even mastery, of the brush. But why a balding fat man in his underwear? Was *George* acquired for subject matter alone? *George* is in the collection simply because *George* is *George.* I am delighted and proud to say that this work could find no better home than our museum.

Talent and technical skill will not exclude work from our gallery. Like *George,* many of the most popular MOBA pieces were made by people with considerable artistic ability that was somehow overshadowed in a particular work by the elusive qualities I look for. Our research department has found that these same artists routinely produce work that would never earn a place in the Museum of Bad Art.

Passion is a key ingredient in bad art, as it is in fine art. In MOBA work, however, feeling often transcends image and assumes the form of simple text, as in *Love Is Being Out on a Limb Together.* Bad artists often feel the need to add written messages to their paintings, just to be sure we don't miss the point.

Size is another of the important criteria I apply when examining a work for MOBA. In general, I must confess that bigger is better.

To my most persistent inquisitors, those who demand a definition of what separates the truly bad from the merely tasteless, large, or incompetent, I direct them to the lady who started it all. *Lucy in the Field with Flowers* has a little of everything I look for in a MOBA painting: some evidence of artistic control, lack of perspective, garish color choices, unusual subject matter, and an inappropriate frame.

While *Lucy* is stunning for combining all of these essentials, the qualities that make her special are evident, at least in part, in all the works accepted into MOBA.

The works in this catalog were chosen to represent the full range and diversity of the permanent collection. It would be easy to think of *Inspiration* simply as a beautiful example of absence of perspective. For unusual subject matter coupled with evidence of artistic control I could refer you to *George*, of course, or to *Mary Todd Lincoln*, *The Athlete*, *And Never the Bride*, *The Cupboard Was Bare*, and *Reef Garden*. There is no doubt that artistic passion outstripped technical skill in *Madonna and Child III*, *Lipstick Twins*, and *The Haircut*.

Yet I resist simplification by categorizing bad art in this way. While pieces may demonstrate a quality I look for, each is uniquely bad in its own terms. In the end, there will always be as many categories as there are works in the collection.

Since my eye first landed on the horn-rimmed squint of *Lucy in the Field with Flowers,* I have spent endless hours squinting at canvas after canvas, rejecting, selecting, and rejoicing in the badness of MOBA acquisitions. As *Lucy* hovers above this collection, I proudly stand behind it.

Sincerely,

Scott Wilson
Curator

# The Museum Of Bad Art

## The Collection

# Lucy in the Field with Flowers

## Artist unknown

24 x 30, Oil on canvas

This single painting planted the seed that grew into MOBA.

The motion, the chair, the expression on her face, the subtle hues of the sky, the sway of her breasts—every detail cries out "masterpiece."

Painted from two photographs of the recently deceased Anna May Lally, this portrait of Ms. Susan Lawlor's maternal grandmother arrived in Ms. Lawlor's home when she was thirteen years old. The piece was commissioned by Ms. Lawlor's mother as a Christmas gift for Ms. Lawlor's aunt, who shared the family home. Ms. Lawlor recalls being startled by the accuracy with which the anonymous artist captured her grandmother's expression and legs. She was equally startled by the setting and by the color of the sky. The portrait hung above the living room mantelpiece until the house was sold in 1989. Ms. Lawlor was vaguely aware of its absence in the new family home, and recalls asking her mother if she knew what happened to the picture of Nanna. The piece had been lost in the move.

In July 1995, Ms. Lawlor was drinking Coca Cola while browsing through a Boston newspaper. Turning the page, she choked, Coke spurting from her nostrils, as she stared at a black-and-white photograph of the seminal piece in the MOBA collection. The museum is profoundly indebted to Ms. Lawlor and her family for their help in piecing together the history of the most important painting in the collection. The painting was found on the street by MOBA's curator in 1993. Its location during the intervening four-year period remains one of MOBA's many mysteries.

## Torment of the Soul

### Artist unknown

22 × 28.5, Acrylic on particleboard

___

An ochre aura emanates from the young man with the eyes of an exorcist. His rhetoric rushes from white joyless lips. His left boot fluoresces above a seething swamp. What happened to his hand?

# When She Grows Up

D. Alix

18 × 24, Acrylic on canvas

A dramatic evocative narrative on the adoration and ambition instilled by a child's first visit to the ballet. A young girl closes her eyes and dreams of her future, dancing for all eternity. Petite, distant, and isolated in time and space, the ballerina *en pointe* will always be the center of attention.

## Pablo Presley

Bonnie Daly

11 × 19.5, Acrylic on paper

Donated by Garen Daly

A refreshing multicultural treatment of one of the twentieth century's most beloved and painted icons.

In late 1995, an Ohio radio station dedicated to collecting likenesses of the late Elvis Presley approached MOBA with an offer to buy *Pablo Presley*. MOBA's curator and executive director argued on the airwaves about the propriety of selling pieces from the MOBA permanent collection. The heated discussion could have resulted in embarrassment to the museum, particularly when the three year old president of Elvis Inc. (the acquisitive subsidiary of WKY) interrupted the MOBA staff to plead for the painting. In a compromise worthy of King Solomon, the curator prompted the station to commission a new painting by Bonnie Daly. Ms. Daly was forced to wrestle with the problem of creating a companion piece without compromising the integrity of the original work.

## And Never the Bride

Artist unknown

25 × 30, Acrylic on canvas

With almost cruel perspicacity, the artist evokes the momentary self-pity of an unmarried eldest sister on her youngest sibling's wedding day. The quaking, the hollow emptiness in the eyes, the self-image shrinking to the tick of the biological clock; old obsessions haunt the consciousness. Despite perfect breasts and long slender hands, it all comes down to heavy thighs. Even the natural linen outfit, in the earth tones she held out for, changes to medieval nunnish garb. A successful career, good friends, and respect of colleagues mean nothing for this moment.

11

## Love Is Being Out on a Limb Together

**Artist unknown**

21 × 24.5, Oil on board

Japanese in its simplicity, American in its text. This valentine in blue hangs in MOBA as a tribute to the poster poems of the seventies.

# The Athlete

Artist unknown

30 × 40, Crayon and pencil on canvas

A startling work, and one of the largest crayon on canvas pieces that most people can ever hope to see. The bulging leg muscles, the black shoes, the white socks, the pink toga, all help to make this one of the most popular pieces in the MOBA collection.

It is hard to believe that this innocent work caused a scandal that threatened to rip MOBA apart in its early years.

*The Athlete* was displayed in our newly opened gallery on the World Wide Web. Within hours electronic missives rained relentlessly on the museum. The piece was identified as a stage prop for the play *You Can't Take It with You* (Moss Hart and George S. Kaufman). Within the context of the play, the work is done by a character who is a bad artist. As such, the piece had been deliberately created as a piece of bad art.

Mr. Wilson, who had personally selected the piece from a trash pile, was called before the board of directors. Wilson was chastised and ordered to remove the work from the permanent collection.

The curator was furious. It has never been proven that it was he who leaked the news of the board's decision to a militant faction within the Friends of the Museum. Overnight "Friends of *The Athlete*" was formed and grew in strength. Its members sported homemade FOTA lapel pins at MOBA public events, and hovered perilously close to members of the press corps in attendance. The faceless, and some say spineless, members of the board bowed to public pressure. The piece was finally reinstated in 1995.

# Inspiration

Artist unknown

24 × 30, Pastels and acrylic on canvas

The organ master stares, transfixed by twin mysterious visions; the Neanderthal saint in the setting sun and the Gothic monk proceeding out from the cathedral's sanctum—each framed by a halo of organ pipes, reminiscent of #2 pencils.

# Madonna and Child III

## A. Fontaine, 1957

16 × 20, Oil on canvas

A work of undisputed tenderness that places the spiritual above the physical through careful disregard for details of the human form.

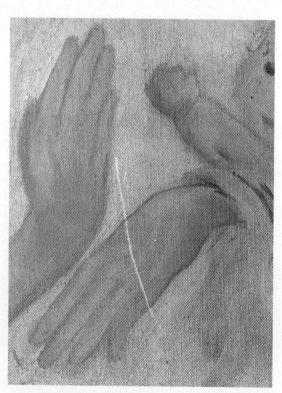

Detail of *Madonna and Child III*

# Mama and Babe

Sarah Irani, 1995

24 × 30, Acrylic on canvas

Donated by the artist

The flesh tones bring to mind the top-shelf liqueurs of a border bistro. With an astonishing emphasis on facial bone structure, the artist flirts with caricature and captures features of Mama's face, reminding us of a First Lady. The upright marionettish pose of the babe hints that the early bond between mother and child is as formal as it is familiar. Good old-fashioned parental respect is at the center of this celebration of color and contour.

Backlit detail of *Mary Todd Lincoln*

# Mary Todd Lincoln

## Frank B. Oldfield

25 × 31, Acrylic and plastic on lace

---

Donated by the artist

The texture of lace lends luster to the complexion. Careful placement of Christmas poinsettias adds an Easter Island element to this remarkable portrait of the sixteenth president's wife.

Painted layer by layer on four sheets of lace and adorned with previously used holiday decorations, this painting was a favorite piece of the artist. Mr. Oldfield presented the work as a gift to a friend and was saddened when it was returned, unwanted. Upon hearing of MOBA and its resolve to provide a home for spectacular and unwanted pieces of art, he was thrilled. "I love it, I would never hang it on my wall, and it seems I can't give it away. Then I heard about MOBA and I rejoiced that there is a place where my painting will be seen and celebrated."

25

# Reef Garden

Hassmer

36 × 36, Mixed media on masonite
in storm window frame

We are witnessing the staging of a
subaqueous musical extravaganza. On
a silent cue, one pulsating incubator
bursts, hurtling an anxious, aged, little
merman upward to the unknown
world above the surface. The dancer
stares, hypnotizing the viewer. We
find ourselves forced to stay, feel the
music, or drown.

# Swamette's Secret

## Artist unknown

30 × 20, Acrylic on canvas

Donated by Patricia Deardorff and
Leigh Weesner

Calm, clear shapes, multiple repeating
patterns, a thickly textured aura, and
little red shoes come together to
conceal or reveal the eternal
complexity of simple truths in this
exploration of the human psyche.

*Swamette's Secret* was donated by Patricia Deardorff
and Leigh Weesner, who purchased the piece for five dollars
from a San Diego thrift store. Neither of these women had
ever been to Boston or had a chance to visit the permanent
gallery. However, they did their homework by studying the
paintings on the Virtual Museum of Bad Art on CD-ROM and
on the MOBA gallery on the World Wide Web. The virtual
sisters then searched for seven months before finding a work
they considered suitable for submission to MOBA. As a
result, they had a painting accepted into the permanent
collection on their first attempt.

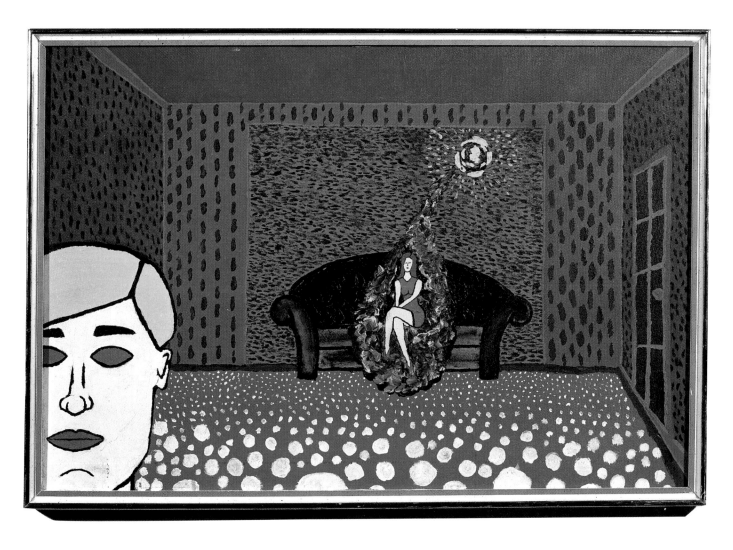

# The Footbridge

## Doug Caderette

16 × 12, Oil, acrylic, lard oil base on canvas

Six identical trees glide silently across the icy terrain to surround the water mill. The brook stops suddenly below the footbridge, holding its breath. What will happen next in this dramatic conflict between man and nature?

# The Horror the Glory

### Tom McKinley, 1952

22 × 26, Acrylic on canvas

Donated by the artist

No detail, and indeed, no man is spared in this bellicose epic. Battle lines reach to the sky itself, where gunsmoke feeds the fury of a storm, imminent in the heavens. Alleluia!

Detail of *The Horror the Glory*

# Eileen

## R. Angelo Le

18 × 24, Acrylic on canvas

---

Remarkable in its simplicity. This passionate portrait of the girl with the green eyes appeals to every emotion. Which passion was uppermost in the painter's breast? Knife stroke follows brush stroke. A hint of a second signature in the top left corner suggests a struggle. An infinitely interesting and sometimes disturbing neoprimitive portrait.

This keynote painting was stolen by a person or persons unknown on the night of March 9, 1996. MOBA has offered a reward of $6.50 for information leading to the recovery of *Eileen*. The reward equals the top price ever paid for a work of art in the permanent collection.

## Madonna with Smile

### Artist unknown

6 × 2 × 1.5, Wood sculpture with felt tip

Much controversy surrounds the history of this piece. Whether the work of a single artist or two artists separated by time and place, the piece succeeds in transforming a simple icon into a mysterious yet radiant image with a few quick dashes of the pen.

## Johnny McGrory

### Anonymous

11 × 14 circumference, Ceramic sculpture

Donated by the artist

With the innocence of an extraterrestrial, his arms in a straitjacket, his flat cap a mortarboard as tribute to his wisdom, the little red man cannot be quieted while something has been left unsaid.

# The Haircut

## M. Jackson and J. Reilly

74 × 28 × 40, Sculpture with barber's chair,
scissors, dental floss, and a piece
of the curator's cat

By special commission for MOBA
opening

Mining the swirling currents between
violence and personal hygiene, this
piece captures the fear, the horror,
and the hope intrinsic in that most
mundane of human activities.

*The Haircut* is possibly the most interactive piece in the
MOBA permanent collection. The notice on the seat below
the scissors reads:

"If you must leave a lock of your hair, please return the
scissors to the center of the seat." It is estimated that one in
five visitors to the gallery donates a lock.

No animal was harmed in the making of this piece.

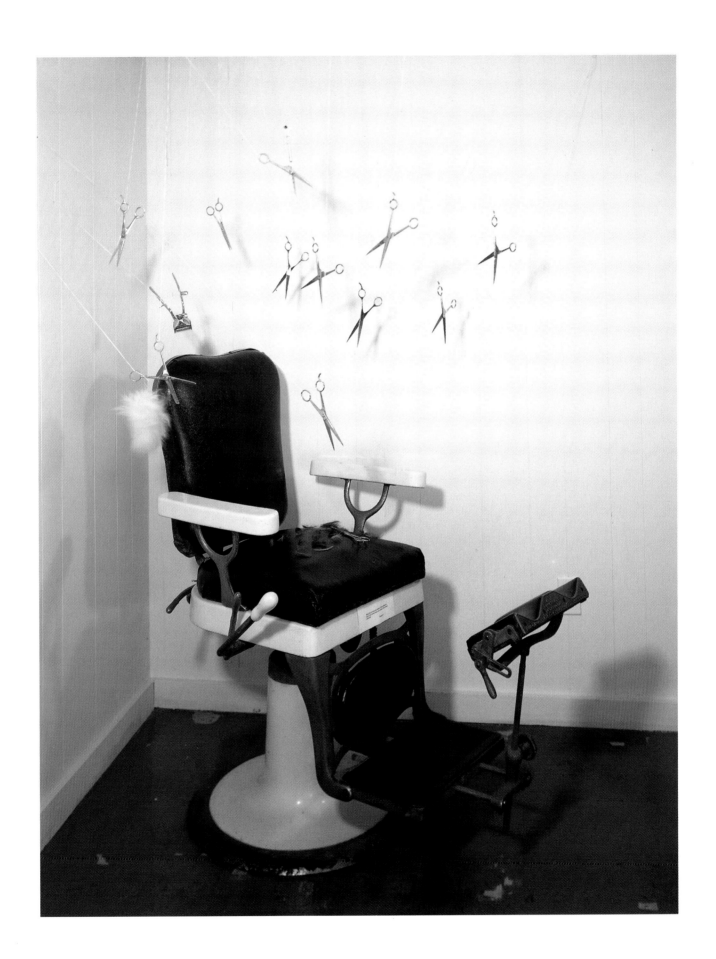

# Red Figure with Braids

## Carlos Rangel

42 × 5 circumference, Painted wood sculpture

A monument to self-confidence. The delicately balanced tiny figure stands tall, leaning towards us in cardinal colors, her pocketbook held proudly at her side. Could this be an ancestor of a late-night television show host?

Detail of *Red Figure with Braids*

## More

Sanford A. Winslow

16 × 20, Acrylic on canvas

All the better to see you with, my dear.

The third eye is the signature of Mr. Winslow's work. Six of his three-eyed portraits were shown at the *I Just Can't Stop/Relentless Creativity* exhibit in the winter of 1996.

# Lipstick Twins

### Aimee Lebec

20 × 16, Acrylic on paper

This artist uses an original daubing technique to echo the levels of skill and enthusiasm of the little girls as they apply the entire contents of their mother's makeup kit to eyelashes, cheeks, and clothes, as well as lips. A masterful recall of the horror of being caught red-handed, the child on the left is poised to blame her sister, whose face is the picture of guilt.

*Lipstick Twins* was presented to the curator, live on television, by Barry Mackerel, host of *The Barry Mackerel Show*. To the unbridled joy of the audience, it was evaluated on the spot by Mr. Wilson, who was a celebrity guest on the show, and immediately accepted into the permanent collection.

## Shy Glance

Artist unknown

18 × 24, Acrylic on canvas

The embarrassment and longing of first love are reflected in the cheek as shiny as an apple, the half-smile hidden behind lank hair.

# Now and Then

### Artist unknown

38 × 38, Acrylic on canvas

Using a double-exposure technique, the artist explores the impact of a rigid world on the female body and spirit over time. The use of a single strong color for walls, chair, nails, and lips comments on the here and now. Yet the past is omnipresent. The outline of a hidden door to the left of the yellow vertical beam bleeds through, and on the subject's face, the smile of former times lingers on paler lips.

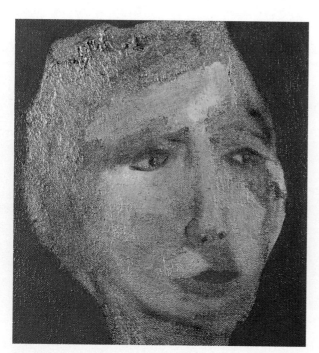

Detail of *Now and Then*

# Below Mt. Washington

Artist unknown

18 × 24, Mixed media on canvas

The choice of colors emphasizes the timeless joy of this quiet, rustic study. Spring bursts from the sapling. Autumn illuminates the more distant view. Whatever the season, the sky is always blue.

## Peter the Kitty

**Artist unknown**

10.5 × 7, Oil on board

Stirring in its portrayal of feline angst. Is Peter hungry or contemplating his place in a hungry world? The artist has evoked both hopelessness and glee with his irrational use of negative space.

We are displaying this favorite of the museum-going public in the condition in which it came to us, because we felt that this book would not be complete if *Peter* were not a part of it. *Peter* has been retired from public exhibition due to its obvious age and frailty. The Friends of MOBA are planning a special fund-raiser to restore *Peter the Kitty* so that it can once again be enjoyed by all.

53

# The Crack of Dawn

## Vickio Saks

18 × 24, Acrylic on canvas

---

Warmed by morning's rays, the shrouded creature uncurls to a world where a solid lake clings to the edge of a mountain. The piece is almost overwhelming in its symbolic content.

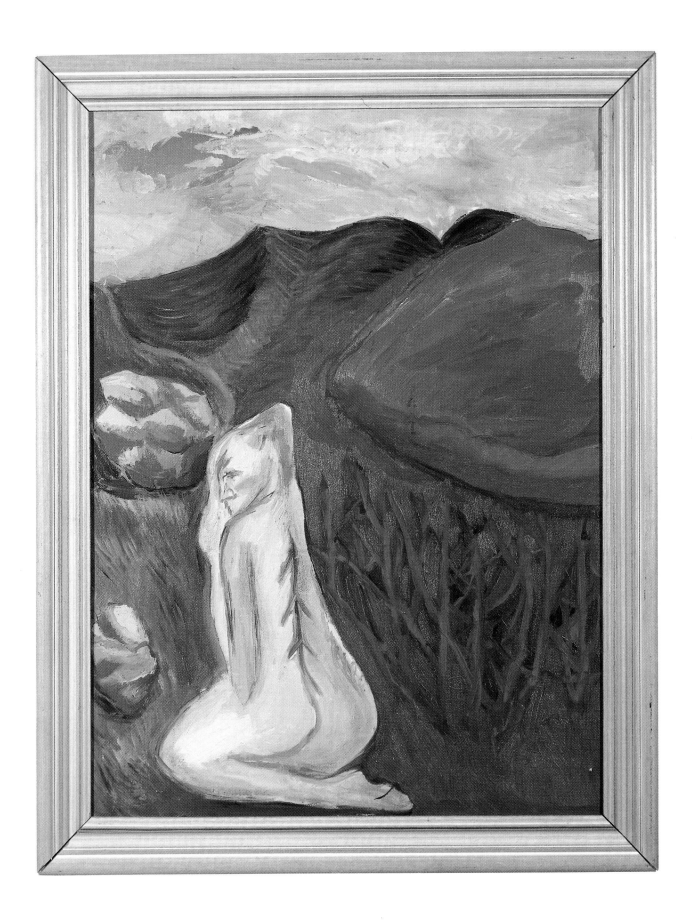

## Pauline Resting

Artist unknown

48 × 21.5, Acrylic on canvas

The cares of the day slip away and the first flush of sleep brings color to Pauline's innocent cheek.

The reverse side of this painting is also interesting. The canvas has been stretched on a basement window frame. When viewed from the obverse, the canvas itself serves as a blind, shielding Pauline from prurient peepers.

# The Departure

H.C. Kimball, 1965

12 × 24, Acrylic on canvas

Through clever use of asymmetry the artist explores the inner conflict about leaving home. The larger left side of the head leans back toward the island, suggesting a longing to stay. The eyes look forward but in two slightly different directions, a reference to confusion about what lies ahead. Drab colors add to the melancholy, but there is hope in the upward springing of the white curl beside the signature, as if to say, "Come on, why the long face?"

-1965-  H.C.Kimball

## Pals

JM, 1966

14 × 18, Acrylic on canvas

A blissful portrayal of deep friendship. The monkey with the Bette Davis eyes chases the blues away, bringing peace to the clown as he grooms his five o'clock shadow.

## Thornton's Pond

### Artist unknown

20 × 24, Mixed media on canvas

The sky exhales a feathery rush,
defying reflection in the murky alpine
waters.

# Janvier

## Hopee

12 × 16, Acrylic on board

Mademoiselle and her petite poodle promenade in the crisp Parisian night. Are they perhaps a little early for a secret rendezvous? Her smile suggests "oui!"

Detail of *The Circus of Despair*

# The Circus of Despair

## Unknown

18 × 24, Oil on canvas

This joyous, frightful circus romp is emblematic of, yet somehow transcends, Unknown's entire body of work.

The Museum of Bad Art is proud and grateful to have in its collection eight works by Unknown. These pieces were shown in the *Bright Colors/Dark Emotions* exhibit at MOBA in the spring of 1994. Four of this prolific artist's works are reproduced in color here.

## Tables Have Turned

Unknown

24 × 18, Acrylic on canvas

The most disturbing piece in this series by Unknown. The anger screams from the canvas, the dysfunctional family fumes after fury's exit left.

## Suicide

### Unknown

18 × 24, Acrylic on canvas

---

Bloody clouds burst in an otherwise
clear sky; froth flies from nostrils as
the bovine beast dives, lemming-like,
and misses the phosphorescent, oily,
swimming hole.

# Under Saba

Unknown

24 × 18, Acrylic on paper

Unknown explores the excitement, danger, and swirling currents in this foray into the gorgeous submarine food chain. This piece is remarkable in the collection for the sheer volume of paint on a single canvas.

# The Cupboard Was Bare

## Pangorda

24 × 30, Mixed media

---

Detail of *The Cupboard Was Bare* with door open

In this complex narrative, the artist addresses how we perceive and the fear of how we are perceived. The faceless female form hesitates. Terror grips the little dog. His left paw pushes, as if to say "You go first." The largest figure lurks behind, holding his pet, but not his mate. The choice of spectacles is confirmation that the artist is conflicted at the prospect of emerging. Yet when the hinged door is opened, we find he has nothing to hide.

*The Cupboard Was Bare* and *In the Cat's Mouth* formed the base of the exhibit *Through the Master's Eyes*, which was unveiled on at least three occasions at MOBA public events. On accepting the entire body of work into the permanent collection, Mr. Wilson was moved to comment, "Not since the *Bright Colors/Dark Emotions* collection have I seen a body of work from a single artist with such a bold and intuitive grasp of everything this museum stands for." The exhibit ran for many months at the permanent gallery, until it was removed by popular demand.

# In the Cat's Mouth

## Probably Pangorda

24 × 22, Acrylic on canvas

A comment on issues of power as experienced by those who dwell with feline pets. Is the artist consumed with or consumed by his love for this cat? Does he identify with the personality of the startling animal? Does the similarity between these inseparable cohabitants stop short at the nose? Or is he simply trying to observe a tree-lined avenue through a cat's eyes?

While this work is unsigned, a weight of evidence supports the theory that it was painted by Pangorda. The artist's whimsical approach, his exploration of the pet and master relationship, is quintessential Pangorda. Finally, this piece was acquired from the same thrift store at the same time as the Pangorda collection.

# Sunday on the Pot with George

### Artist unknown

22 × 37, Acrylic on canvas

Donated by Mr. Jim Schulman

Can the swirling steam melt away the huge weight of George's corporate responsibilities? The pointillist piece is curious for meticulous attention to fine detail, such as the stitching around the edge of the towel, coupled with the almost careless disregard for the subject's feet.

This work is notable as the first unsolicited donation by a Friend of the Museum. Mr. Jim Schulman acquired this breathtaking pointillist piece at an auction ten years ago and had been wondering what to do with it when news of the newly founded MOBA reached him. The office staff urged him to submit a photograph of the work to our curator for preliminary consideration. Mr. Schulman insisted on sending the painting by courier, although he was fully aware of our no-return policy. Mr. Wilson received the shipment, muttering his irritation at the breach of submission guidelines even as his well-manicured hands clawed open the box. The staff held its collective breath. A whisper broke the interminable silence. "Oh my word! It's in—for subject matter alone," Wilson gasped. The tiny multitude rejoiced at the rare opportunity to have communed, however briefly, with the discerning taste of Mr. Wilson.

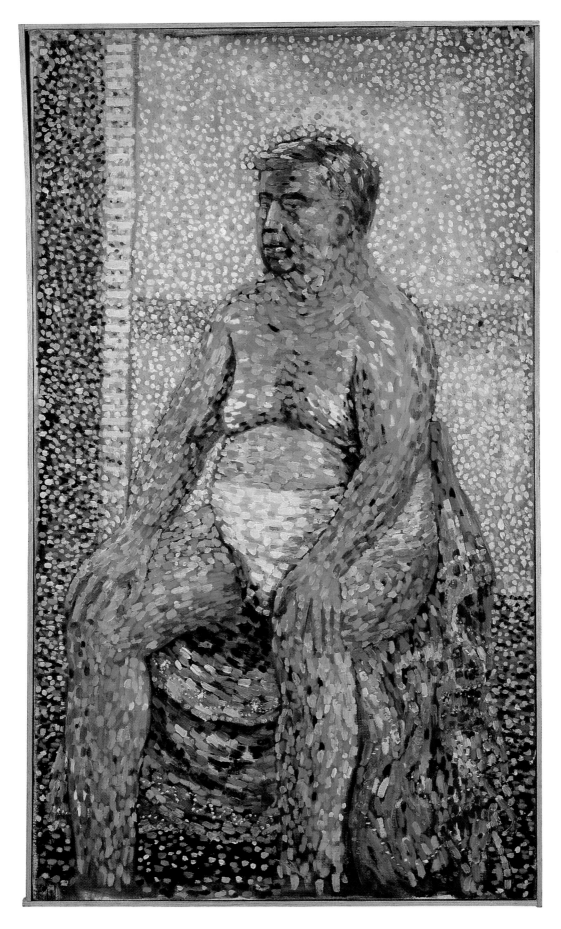

# Frequently Asked Questions about the Museum of Bad Art

**Q:** *Is the Museum of Bad Art real or does it only exist in a virtual way?*

**A:** The Museum of Bad Art is very real. Our permanent collection of over one hundred pieces is stored in our World Headquarters in Boston. Through our Public Events program we continually strive to find new and creative ways to bring the collection to the public, in both our outdoor and indoor galleries. Our permanent gallery in Dedham, Massachusetts, displays a rotating selection of the collected works. Two virtual galleries have been established on the World Wide Web at http://glyphs.com/MOBA/. The Virtual Museum of Bad Art exists on CD-ROM and features sixty works of art and ninety-two friends of MOBA. Visitors to MOBA's real and virtual exhibitions are the most engaged museum patrons you will find anywhere. Every one is an expert on bad art. MOBA's supporters constantly second-guess, critique, and object to our curator's decisions. Rather than taking this as an insult, Mr. Wilson and the staff see it as a sign of MOBA's astonishing vitality.

**Q:** *Is this some kind of a joke?*

**A:** This institution works long and hard at building the finest bad art establishment in the world. We take our mission very seriously. Frankly, we are shocked and indignant at your derisive innuendo.

**Q:** *Why no velvet Elvis?*

**A:** A large number of our pieces come to us from the public refuse system. Our first task is dealing with safety issues, including removal of any pointed edges, broken glass, or parasites. We have a particular problem with works on velvet, as the velvet may have become impregnated with animal body fluids after leaving a previous owner and before reaching us. We find it challenging to remove any bacterial growths from this particular fabric without causing damage to the art itself. We encourage those who collect art of this nature from more pristine sources to open their own museums and make the work available to the public.

**Q:** *Where is my luggage?*

**A:** The Museum of Bad Art is proud to share the same telephone number as Delta Airlines Information. More than a few Friends of MOBA discovered the museum when they neglected to dial the 1-800 prefix.

**Q:** *With the growing popularity of bad art, are you afraid that fine arts museums will open bad art sections?*

**A:** Our mission is to bring this work to the public and we welcome help from all quarters. If this were to happen, we would be thrilled and would take it as a sign of a job well done.

# The Museum Of Bad Art

## The Institution

## From Humble Beginnings

The founding of a museum is a serious undertaking, so it is difficult to believe that this wondrous institution magically brought itself into being, as if by accident. In 1993, Mr. Scott Wilson, a Boston antique dealer, spotted a frame protruding from between two trash barrels on a curbside. He took it home, unaware of the treasure within: a painting so powerful it commands its own preservation for posterity. Was it truly by accident that Wilson "found" *Lucy in the Field with Flowers?* Or did *Lucy* find him?

*Lucy* is a spectacular work. It is painted with such courage, confidence, and conviction that even unseen, in the dark, it silently cried out to Wilson, "Take me! Take me home and display me." Powerless, he obeyed.

Several weeks later, on the very day *Lucy* demanded to be taken down from the attic, Jerry Reilly and Marie Jackson visited the Wilson home on impulse. The moment they saw the painting, they found themselves begging to be allowed to take it and hang it in their home. The work had wielded its influence a second time.

Two weeks later, Wilson found a second piece as powerful as the first. He felt suddenly compelled to drive straight to his friend's home, as if directed there by the painting itself. *Eileen* was taken to *Lucy.*

A pact was made on the spot. Wilson was to collect the art and Reilly and Jackson would find a way to make the work available to the public. The Museum of Bad Art had come into being, its mission commanded by the work itself. MOBA must bring the worst of art to the widest of audiences.

The following spring, in the basement of the Reilly–Jackson home in a quiet Boston neighborhood, twenty-two pieces were mounted on freshly painted white walls above a plain gray floor. A card

> **"These works of art ought to be in a museum."**
>
> – Scott Wilson

*Lucy* lurks in wait for Wilson.

The site of the first MOBA Gallery.

bearing the title and a short commentary on the finer points of the piece accompanied each work of art. When everything was ready for viewing, family, friends, neighbors, and a few strangers poured in to attend the opening of the Museum of Bad Art.

The opening exhibition had been planned as a small, private affair. However, as each person departed, another arrived. Attendance far exceeded the invitation list, as if each painting brought its own followers. One hundred and fifty signatures filled the opening pages of the guest book, many indecipherable, many unknown to the founders.

The founding of MOBA is filled with accidental encounters, strange coincidences, and a mysterious momentum. These pages outline the growth of the fledgling museum and its development into one of the most remarkable and unique arts institutions of the late twentieth century.

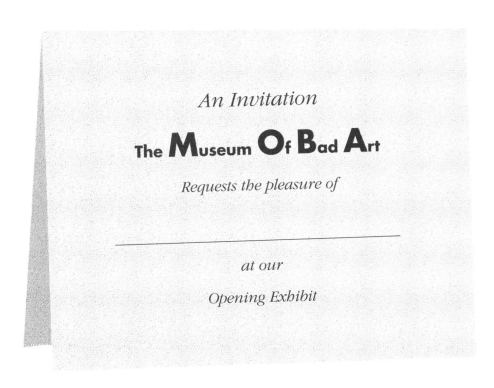

*An Invitation*

The **M**useum **O**f **B**ad **A**rt

*Requests the pleasure of*

_____

*at our*

*Opening Exhibit*

## The Public Exhibition Program

In the early days of the Museum of Bad Art, the main challenge to the founders was finding ways to bring the art to the public.

Throughout 1994, the museum held a series of exhibitions in its basement gallery.

Scott Wilson, as MOBA's newly appointed Esteemed Curator, continued to add to the collection, finding wonderful works at yard sales and flea markets, never paying more than the agreed six dollars and fifty cents for a single piece.

News of the museum spread quickly. Jerry Reilly took the helm as Executive Director, and set up MOBA World Headquarters. The office was immediately swamped with calls from supporters, pleading to be admitted into the Friends of MOBA and to receive invitations to all exhibitions.

The arrival of a huge bequest from the public refuse system brought to a head a crisis facing the fledgling museum. The pace of acquisition had clearly outstripped the meager exhibition space at the basement gallery. The future of the museum was uncertain when the Friends of MOBA came forward with a bold new plan to guide the institution into the twenty-first century.

The opening of *Bright Colors/Dark Emotions,* the final exhibit at the basement gallery, was the springboard that launched the next phase of the Public Exhibition program.

Hundreds flocked to the gallery on the night the final show opened. A line formed outside the front door, down the steps, along the path, even as far as the street. It seemed as though every Friend of MOBA had brought a friend, or two, or three.

For MOBA's patrons it was worth the wait to see *The Circus of Despair, Tables Have Turned, Under Saba,* and *Suicide,* with other works by Unknown.

---

*On a cool, windy night, Scott Wilson, MOBA curator, came upon a discovery that would change his life and the future of this museum.*

*"It was big, I just didn't know how big," said Wilson, recalling the moment of the discovery.*

*He ordered the car to stop. "Back up," he screamed.*

*As he leapt from the car, the topmost painting blew from the pile. The one below was even worse! One, two . . . seven, eight . . . each one worse than the last.*

*"I laughed, I wept, I danced in the street."*

*"What is it? Who did them?" called a voice from the car.*

*"It's unknown," Scott replied, "It's Unknown."*

---

## The Museum Of Bad Art

*is proud to present*

### Bright Colors/Dark Emotions

by the artist Unknown

Crowds swarm to the tiny basement gallery.

Inside the house, the plan that would save MOBA was put into action. Each patron was invited to participate in building a huge new facility with galleries, a café, a gift shop—everything one would expect of a world-class institution. Patrons who signed up for the project then visited the photographic studio on the second floor, where Tom Stankowicz, the museum's Head of Imaging and Reproduction, took portrait photographs. Across the hall in the sound studio, Nancy Jurcoic, Director of Public Outreach, interviewed the teeming masses.

The patrons imagined themselves in the museum of the future, and described their reason for being there. They talked about the art and each other. One worked in the café, several in the office, two were security guards, the majority were visitors. Each invented a character, and suddenly there were gardens with a groundskeeper, a shipping room with a shipper, and a truck driver making deliveries.

Each agreed to a one-day location shoot in the near future. The new facility was about to be built on CD-ROM.

Upstairs in MOBA's photography studio, a Friend of MOBA signs up to help save the museum.

The MOBA Board of Directors initially balked at the proposal to build a facility with a stone facade, a grand lobby, six galleries, a restaurant and gift shop, and enough additional space to allow adequate expansion of the administration department. When they finally grasped the concept of a CD-ROM, the board unanimously voted in favor.

The production had the atmosphere of an old-fashioned barn raising. The ever-growing Friends of MOBA flocked to lend locations, computers, and recording equipment, as well as their time, talent, and expertise. Dozens of new characters were developed during improvisation sessions. Editing and authoring took place at nights and on weekends while location shoots and sound recording filled the days. West Coast friends of MOBA sent designs for the cover. Friends from around the country sent enough electronic images to fill a bulletin board. A child wrote the MOBA anthem. Days later, the newly formed MOBA chorus recorded the piece.

The CD-ROM, completed in June 1995, was unique among virtual museums. Sixty pieces of spectacularly bad art hung in the twenty-four-room facility, which was crowded with ninety-two characters aged two to eighty-two. Once again, the Museum of Bad Art has a public exhibition space where it could bring the worst of art to the widest of audiences, in their own homes, schools, and offices.

## The Virtual Museum of Bad Art

"...full of chatty outrageous characters"

— Wired Magazine

"unique showcase of canvas calamities"

— Sky Magazine

"A complete waste of plastic"

— Computer Currents

"Cheaper than the Louvre - and more laughs."

— CD-ROM Today

"Ironic celebration of creative incompetence"

— Rolling Stone

*"I could swear, on my mother's grave, I've done her hair before."*

—Judy Collins, hairdresser, recalls her reaction to *Lucy*

*"I've seen bad art in some of the best museums in the world, but this place is full of it."*

—Lorraine McGrath, visitor in lobby

*"I was very impressed with some of the frames. What's inside the frame is less important."*

—Peter O'Reilly, visitor in lobby

*"I like the colors, I like the red, the blue, and the yellow."*

—Theresa O'Connell, admiring *Pauline Resting*

*"Quite often the paintings are covered with dust or other coatings. Years of cigarette smoke can really put a patina on a painting. I tend to use water as a solvent, and I scrub a lot with a toothbrush and the natural sponge."*

—Ethan Berry, conservator

## The MOBA News

Since its founding, members of the public have sought out the Museum of Bad Art, cheering it on and hoping that somehow its existence would enable them to exchange views with others who share an appreciation of bad art.

Working with limited resources, MOBA resolved to find creative ways to enable the celebration of bad art to continue, meanwhile seeking a physical exhibition space. The most urgent challenge was to create a flow of news and information. With guidance from the executive director, the board agreed to commit staff time and resources to the creation of the *MOBA News*.

With a circulation of close to two thousand, the official organ of the Museum of Bad Art is delivered via the Internet to bad art enthusiasts on six continents, proving the executive director's long-held belief that bad art exists wherever humankind lives.

In the hectic days of making the Virtual Museum, the newsletter was published weekly, carrying full details of progress on the CD-ROM project. A cutback in the number of issues per year brought sadness to some readers, but successfully raised the quality of the newsletter. News is garnered from its readers as well as from within the museum.

Excerpts of *MOBA News* articles are used throughout these pages to convey the inimitable style and flavor of MOBA events. The number of issues published yearly remains a closely guarded secret.

---

Boston, MA

No Newsletter?

HERE IT IS (yes I am yelling) AFTER NOON TIME AND I HAVE YET TO FIND OUT WHAT HAS BEEN GOING ON IN THE WORLD OF MOBA THIS PAST WEEK. WHEN I COMMIT MYSELF AND MY FAMILY TO AN ORGANIZATION I EXPECT THAT ORGANIZATION TO BE COMMITTED TO ME. ARE YOU HEARING THIS?

How are we—the little guys out here in a world full of bad art—supposed to sustain that energy level that will bring this organization universal recognition?

I WANT NEWS. I want good news about Bad stuff. I want anecdotes, I want downloads from the wire services. I am going to be under a lot of pressure if I go home tonight without an update. What do I tell the children —that it was all a hoax? That the museum is no more than a bunch of electrons that no one can control or understand? They don't want to hear that. The very fabrik of their day to day pleasure with living depends on the knowledge that MOBA has established a solid foundation from which they can go forth into a world full of pain, suffering and dispair and be able to function as somewhat sane humanoids.

This is not a minor screwup—this is more than just giving out the wrong date for virtually every event that you have ever staged. Get it together or give it up and let us off. Tell us its over now if you must—slam the door—burn ruber on the way out of town, but DON'T try to ease out of your responsibility and kill us softly. Just shoot to kill for Godsake!

John O'Connell

---

Dear Mr. O'Connell

Thank you for your misspelled and ungrammatical letter. The MOBA News will henceforth be published with less frequency than before. We want to assure you that no one here at MOBA has any firearms and we mean you no harm.

Sincerely
Jerry Reilly
Executive Director

## Points Review

Compares Museum Web Sites

Scores out of 50

|  | Museum of Bad Art | The Louvre |
|---|---|---|
| Content | 32 | 34 |
| Presentation | 30 | 36 |
| Experience | 35 | 34 |

# The MOBA Gallery on the World Wide Web

The Museum of Bad Art was established during a period of severe cutbacks in funding for the arts. It quickly adopted a policy of frugality.

The museum trained its staff in the creative use of the cheapest resources available, to solicit donations of bad art. Development Committee members distributed literature on the Outreach to Artists program during the 1995 Annual Appeal for Submissions. The literature was posted to artists' newsgroups on the Internet, saving thousands of dollars in postage. Sadly, no bad art was acquired. However, as a result of this initiative, Bob Stewart, managing editor of the *Virtual Mirror,* a magazine on the World Wide Web, contacted the museum. Mr. Stewart generously offered MOBA a page in his magazine. With board approval, the executive director established a new exhibition space on the web page, providing bad art enthusiasts with a cultural stop on the Infobahn.

Visitors will find a selection of works from the MOBA permanent collection and supporting literature at

## http://www.glyphs.com/moba/

The outstanding success of the MOBA page, which is updated biannually, is reflected in the Comparative Report on Web Sites carried out by *Points Review,* an on-line review of museum web sites.

## The Public Awareness Program

The Museum of Bad Art's Public Awareness program was devised to bring the institution into the public eye.

On July 7, 1995, months of work paid off when an article on the Museum of Bad Art and a reproduction of *Eileen* graced the front page of *The Wall Street Journal.* The reporter, Jim Hirsch, had read of MOBA in *Wired* magazine. *Wired* magazine read of MOBA in *MOBA News.*

In the following months our esteemed curator and executive director selflessly put themselves at the disposal of the MOBA Media Relations Department. They were interviewed first by WCVB, WBZ, and WHDH News in Boston. *CBS This Morning,* and the *Today Show* soon brought MOBA to a national audience. International exposure followed, with coverage on CNN News, and German and Australian television, culminating in guest appearances on Somerville Cable Access Television's *The Barry Mackerel Show.*

Mr. Wilson allowed a *People* magazine photographer to wrap him like a mummy, confident that the bizarre image would cause an influx of submissions from the rest of the nation. The fruits of this campaign include the arrival of *Sunday on the Pot with George* from Pennsylvania, *Mary Todd Lincoln* from Georgia, *The Horror the Glory* from Virginia, and *Mama and Babe* from Arizona.

"Gosh, that's awful! It would look great hanging in a museum."
— The Wall Street Journal

"They're not in it for the Monet"
— People magazine

"At The Museum Of Bad Art, failure finds a happy home."
—Boston Sunday Globe

"If art is a gas, this museum is a stinker."
— The Oregonian

"Museum of Bad Art is awful big success"
— London Sunday Times

Months of media madness at MOBA resulted in submissions from coast to coast.

The Public Events program differs from the Public Exhibition program in that it aims to bring MOBA art out to the people, whereas the exhibition program concentrates its efforts within the confines of MOBA's galleries.

## Public Events Program

Artist Bonnie Daly chats about *Pablo Presley* to an Australian TV crew.

The two departments work closely together, juggling logistics of where each piece of art will be shown, how frequently new pieces will be unveiled, and at what locations. The crowning example of teamwork between the departments was the First Annual Gallery in the Woods Gala held in August 1995 in Wellfleet, Massachusetts, "Cape Cod's Gallery Town." The boundless exhibition space allowed the entire permanent collection to be seen in one place at one time.

*Art Goes out the Window* at the Gallery in the Woods.

MOBA has forged strong relationships with private collectors willing to lend works for exhibition. Renowned collector Ollie Hallowell received the honor of being the first MOBA guest exhibitor. The occasion provided MOBA with the opportunity to allow work normally unseen by the public to be viewed by hordes returning from the beach.

The proximity of the exhibition space to a tent paradise prompted the inclusion of an affordable and intimate weekend retreat, where travelers could immerse themselves in bad art in a community atmosphere for two days.

Ollie Hallowell, guest exhibitor at the Gallery in the Woods.

# The MOBA News

Issue #25

Bad Art Takes Cape Cod By Storm—
The First Annual MOBA Gallery in the Woods was a spectacular success. Friends Of MOBA began arriving at Paine's Campground in Wellfleet on Thursday afternoon to set up the MOBA Group Encampment and transfer the entire permanent collection from the MOBA van into the huge (temperature-controlled) MOBA security tent.

On Saturday, an Australian Broadcast TV crew captured the construction effort as part of its story about the museum. An exuberant MOBA team ran hundreds of feet of electrical and audio cable through the woods, hung banners and flags, set up three complete computer systems, refreshment tables, and the MOBA Gift Shop, and mounted the massive exhibit.

Minutes before the 5 PM opening, the final touches were completed just in time for the MOBA crew to change into its finest garb. The eagerly awaiting crowds wound down the dirt road from the entrance rope, back to the campground parking lot.

Gloriously attired in tuxedos, gold lamé, party dresses, T-shirts, jeans, and bathing suits, they came from MA, RI, NH, CT, VT, NY, NJ, VA, IL, France, Italy, Austria, and England. Among the guests was Susan Lawlor who brought her nephew, Mark Hedstrom, for his first viewing of his maternal grandmother, immortalized in *Lucy in the Field with Flowers.* Bonnie Daly, one of the few known MOBA artists, came with her family. Her masterpiece, *Pablo Presley,* had a place of honor at the entrance to the Gallery in the Woods.

The Gallery itself was breathtaking. Eighty-five paintings and sculptures were proudly displayed along a twisting dirt road. Bad music played from hidden speakers along the route. In a side gallery, guest exhibitor Ollie Hallowell displayed wondrous works from the Hallowell Collection, featuring spectacular pieces that are outside of MOBA's realm—including a number of choice velvet paintings.

After a hectic program of speeches and the unveiling of new acquisitions, 11-year-old Sheila Reilly led the assembled multitude in a rousing rendition of the anthem "MOBA MOBA" to close the exhibition at about 7 PM.

The Friends of MOBA took only an hour to disassemble the Gallery in the Woods, and safely place the permanent collection in the temperature-controlled tent. Then all sat, sighed, and relaxed over a wonderful dinner catered by Aileen Cormier, MOBA's cook extraordinaire.

It is essential for an arts institution to make regular contact with all sections of the community it serves. When Montserrat College of Art in Beverly, Massachusetts, asked MOBA to exhibit in their streetfront gallery, the board immediately accepted the invitation.

The large plate-glass window encouraged not only campus traffic, but passersby from the local area, so that the MOBA exhibit was viewed by two sections of the community in one location.

After a resoundingly successful opening, the show, titled *Know What You Like, Paint How You Feel,* ran for two weeks. For the first time, the MOBA exhibit and the works of individual MOBA paintings were reviewed by art critics from local newspapers. Previous press coverage of the museum had, for some reason, been written by news reporters.

MOBA's policy of banning obvious student work may have alienated this section of the arts community in the past. This show provided MOBA staff with an opportunity to assure students that the museum viewed them as their greatest resource for the future. The executive director was enthusiastic in his encouragement of submissions from faculty members. As part of MOBA's Educational Outreach program, the curator addressed faculty and students, using pieces from his reject pile to differentiate between mediocre, bad, and museum-quality bad art.

# MOBA Goes to School

## *Know What You Like, Paint How You Feel*
### at Montserrat College of Art

Artist Aimee LeBec unveils her painting.

## Bad Art A Delightful Exhibit.

"Montserrat's Museum Of Bad Art (MOBA) exhibit, an exuberant celebration of artistic failure, is not to be missed by anyone who has ever painted."

— Salem Evening News

# The MOBA News

Issue #27

Academic Accolades—MOBA took Beverly, MA by storm last Friday night. MOBA's latest show—"Know what you like/paint how you feel" presented a cross section of MOBA's permanent collection along with the MOBA Virtual Museum CD-ROM at the Cabot Gallery at Montserrat College Of Art.

In spite of miserable weather, approximately 200 people turned up at the former furniture store for a firsthand look at MOBA's exhibition. After opening remarks by Ethan Berry and our Executive Director, the enthusiastic crowd toured the gallery and noshed on the plentiful foods, generously supplied by our hosts at the college—peanut butter, raspberry fluff, Spam, and gallons of fluorescent (is there any other kind) colored Kool-Aid.

Later in the evening, as part of MOBA's ongoing educational program, our esteemed curator led the public through a few of the more interesting pieces that have recently been rejected by MOBA. Mr. Wilson explained the curatorial process involved with each rejection, highlighting the sometimes subtle attributes that can keep a piece out of MOBA's permanent collection. He showed a few pieces that a lesser curator of bad art might let slip by. The gallery crowd seemed to particularly enjoy this display of "close but not cigar" works, and the opportunity to appreciate the sublime shadings involved in the curator's finely tuned judgments.

At one point, Montserrat's gallery director, Barbara O'Brien, and a member of the public whom she had just met, spontaneously took to the stage and introduced a presentation entitled "Top ten reasons to collect bad art." As it turned out, they only had two reasons, but all in attendance agreed—it was a good start.

Later still, five exceptional new additions to the permanent collection were unveiled to the eagerly awaiting audience.

*Taiarapu*—a brooding Indian girl, rendered in many shades of chocolate.

*The Horror the Glory*—an epic battle scene with a cast of thousands.

*Lipstick Twins*—The artist, Aimee LeBec, was on hand to pull back the veil of her joyous and confused image of the lipstick smeared little girls. This painting was a generous gift to MOBA from the world renown hosts of the Somerville Community Access TV's Barry Mackeral Show—Barry Mackeral and Paul Leonard.

*Jerez the Clown*—a startling portrait of a clown with a satanic glare. This proved to be the most controversial of the new additions.

*Sid's Birthday*—A huge canvas, possibly part of a massive tryptich, that captures the face, portion of his head, and very very long neck of Sid, all bathed in light from an unseen, off canvas birthday cake.

When the reception ended, everyone was invited to The Red Raven restaurant in nearby Salem, where the MOBA denizens continued their revelry until the wee hours while the MOBA Directors were whisked away to WBZ radio studios for a late night visit with talk show host Norm Nathan.

MOBA extends our heartfelt apologies to the two "bad cartoonists from Albany" that found the exhibit closed on Sat afternoon and left a note on the door. The attendant had closed the gallery for a short time so he could get his lunch. We're very sorry for any inconvenience it caused.

# The MOBA Permanent Gallery

For many months after the closing of the original basement gallery at the Jackson-Reilly home, the Museum of Bad Art faced the challenges of exhibiting without a space.

In October 1995, cinema owner Garen Daly offered MOBA a space in the basement of one of his theaters. Mr. Daly is a longtime, close friend of MOBA, the tour guide on the Virtual Museum, and donor of *Pablo Presley*.

The gallery, on inspection, was perfect, large enough to display up to thirty pieces of art. The location close to the men's room offered the advantage of passing traffic and built-in humidity control.

The cinema is in the center of town, with ample parking and within reach of downtown Boston via public transportation.

In return for his generosity, MOBA provides Mr. Daly's theater with art exhibits unequaled in the cinema history of the country.

Members of a German television crew assisted in setting up the first exhibit. A sneak preview on the *Today Show* was permitted by the board of directors.

Attendance at the permanent gallery is high, ranging from cinemagoers and school trips to international visitors to New Englanders. Although the owners of MOBA's original exhibition space feel there is something missing in their basement, they are thrilled that the opening of *I Just Can't Stop—Relentless Creativity* in the spring of 1996 had the largest attendance in MOBA history . . . to date.

## The MOBA News
### Issue # 31

Extravaganza in Dedham—MOBA's new gallery in the basement of the Dedham Community Theater opened on Monday, Oct. 30, amid much excitement and fanfare.

By special permission of the MOBA board of directors, the Today Show was allowed in for a sneak preview of the exhibition. On Monday evening, the crowds arrived to a festive atmosphere in Dedham Square.

As the lobby began to overflow with the multitudes, waiting to descend to the MOBA Gallery—a cheer went up from the crowd. The arrival of the special surprise guests—The Dedham High School Cheerleaders.

Garen Daly, MOBA's host at the theater, used the opportunity to highlight the key difference between his theater and the national chain 100 screen multiplex up the road. His theater has real art by real people, theirs has mass produced reproductions.

Next, the cheerleading squad marched across the lobby holding the ceremonial scissors proudly above their captain's head as they approached the Gallery entrance. With one deft and graceful motion, the captain brought the scissors down from on high, cut the ribbon, and the crowd poured through the entrance, down the stairs and into the new MOBA Gallery.

Once inside the overflow crowd immersed themselves joyously in the representative sample of MOBA's permanent collection.

Later, Mr. Wilson announced the world premier of a startling series of five paintings entitled "Through the Master's Eyes."

As our curator introduced each piece in the series, the MOBA bowling team (Men On Bowling Alleys) *in perfect coordination* with the Dedham High Cheerleaders, pulled back the veil to reveal each canvas to the awestruck public— each one more powerful than the last—each one adding to the whole.

MOBA art en route to the new permanent gallery.

November 10

Dear Mr. Reilly,
. . . We were able to go to MOBA Sunday and
it was FANTASTIC! . . . The two paintings that
spoke to me the most were "Peter the Kitty"
and "Janvier" —the woman and her poodle.
That was bad art that warmed my soul. The
most dramatic effect, however came while I
was studying "Sunday on the Pot With
George." Someone had slipped into the
bathroom as I took in this painting and began
to pee loudly into a toilet. The reverberating
sound of urine splashing while viewing
"George" brought the painting to life, and
when the denouement of the flush sounded, I
wept . . .

Sincerely,
Gary R. Hunnicutt

MOBA artist Alan Collins at the opening of
*I Just Can't Stop — Relentless Creativity.*

MOBA artist Sanford Winslow displays his work at *I Just Can't Stop — Relentless Creativity.*

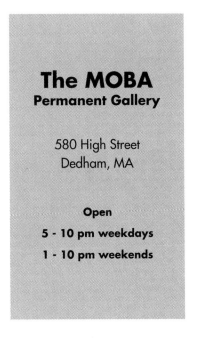

**The MOBA**
**Permanent Gallery**

580 High Street
Dedham, MA

**Open**
**5 - 10 pm weekdays**
**1 - 10 pm weekends**

## Submission Guidelines

*Before* submitting work for possible acceptance into MOBA's permanent collection, please take a moment to read these simple guidelines.

- **Nine out of ten submissions to the Museum of Bad Art are rejected.**

- **Rejected works are used for educational purposes at MOBA public events. Accepted pieces become part of the permanent collection. They are unveiled regularly and may be displayed at MOBA galleries and traveling exhibitions.**

- **As the founding principle of the museum is the celebration of the right to fail, we strongly urge you to submit and resubmit. No human emotion can match the joy of having a piece accepted into the MOBA collection.**

- **All submissions go before the subjective scrutiny of Mr. Scott Wilson, whose decision is final. No amount of lobbying will change his mind. Argument is pointless and treated with disdain.**

- **The only promise MOBA makes to those who submit work is that we will never send it back.**

## Work must be original and show one or more of the following:

- complete artistic control

- no artistic control

- courage and enthusiasm

- unusual use of color

- interesting use of perspective

- strange subject matter

- an inappropriate frame

- MOBA is actively seeking three-dimensional art

---

"appears to have promise"

— Scott Wilson

Submissions should be shipped to

### The **M**useum **O**f **B**ad **A**rt
**10 Vogel Street**
**Boston MA 02132**

All shipping charges are the responsibility of the donor.
We recommend that you first submit a photograph of the work.

## Work in the following categories will be rejected:

- reproductions

- works on velvet

- paint-by-numbers

- factory or mass-produced art

- obvious student exercises

- deliberately made bad art

- bad craftwork, crocheted rugs, etc.

"Tacky as hell, but far too much craft"

— Scott Wilson

"Too Competent"

— Scott Wilson

"Way too ugly! Get it out of here"

— Scott Wilson

"Genius! It's in."

— Scott Wilson

MEMO

To: MOBA

Re: OBJECTION

"The Landscape With The Velvet Cloud", "a most unusual landscape" was rejected because of MOBA's inveterate, dogmatic "ban on paint-by-number", despite the fact it was a painting "in which all the wrong numbers had been used". I am quoting the very words used in the MOBA News.

INDIGNATION: think about a man/woman — that revolutional charactor, who dared to spit at the servile instruction and used colors prompted by his/her imagination! She/he was possibly a color-blind man/woman, but not a hack-worker like that woman/man Picasso (a Frenchman/Frenchwoman, we guess) who confessed (according to quote in MOBA News) to using red when she/he was out of blue.

DEMAND: Open a branch of the museum for the paintings with certain merits, but rejected by the main MOBA.

RESPONSIBILITY: MOBA Officials

The Hoffmans

Dear Mr. and Mrs. Hoffman,

While we applaud your suggestion to open a "Museum Of Not Quite Bad Art" we don't believe that this is in any way our responsibility. We of course would support such an effort in principle. MOBA has always urged anyone who disagreed with our curatorial decisions to open their own museum.

We believe we have fulfilled our responsibilities to your family by making good on the one promise that our acquisition dept makes to all MOBA donors, i.e. whether or not a work is accepted to the MOBA collection, we promise to never return it to the donor.

Sincerely
Jerry Reilly

# The Friends of MOBA

*The Friends of MOBA* are as many and varied as the sands on the shore. Already spanning six continents, they are united in their generosity of spirit and selfless dedication to the principles of the museum.

### Advantages of membership

- A subscription to the *MOBA News*

- Celebrity status

- Invitations to all public and private museum events

- The chance to play on the MOBA softball team

- The opportunity to cheer on the MOBA bowling team (Men On Bowling Alleys)

- Personal pride and satisfaction in supporting the work of this illustrious institution

- Inclusion on the MOBA mailing list

- It's free

### Friends of MOBA must

- Celebrate bad art

- Honor MOBA and uphold its principles

- Demonstrate willingness to travel across many states to support MOBA events*

**If you think you have what it takes to be a Friend of MOBA, please photocopy and fill out the form on the opposite page.**

*Actual travel is not required, it is the wish to be there that counts.

Members of the Boston Chapter of the Friends of MOBA take the art out for a walk in the sun.

# Join the Friends of MOBA

*"I wish to be considered for membership in the Friends of MOBA. I solemnly swear/promise that henceforth my life will be dedicated to the collection, celebration and preservation of bad art. I support the principles on which MOBA was founded and will uphold its standards and honor its name.*

Signature _____

Name _____

Address _____

_____

Town _____ State _____ Zip _____

e-mail address _____

Telephone _____ Fax _____

Favorite color _____

Mail to:

**The Museum Of Bad Art**
**10 Vogel Street**
**Boston MA 02132**

or send the following e-mail message to
MOBA-news-request@WORLD.STD.COM
subscribe

| | | | | |
|---|---|---|---|---|
| Susan Abbott | Andrew Berish | Joe Carmichael | Patricia Dains | Chuck Emery |
| Wendy Abraham | Suzanne Bernard | Ruth Carney | Martin Dalgleish | Bob Emory |
| Mark Abrahams | Beverly Benson | John Carpenter | Bill Dalton | Joe Enright |
| John Abreau | Ethan Berry | Tyler Carpenter | Bonnie Daly | Jeremy Epworth |
| Chris Ackerman | Chris Besser | Francis Carr | Garen Daly | Nancy Errebo |
| Levi Adams | Nancie Bestwick | M H Carr | Graham Daly | Duane Esbenshade |
| Thomas Adams | Joe Beyer | Daniel Carroll | Jeff Dames | Glenn Escott |
| Vicki Adleman | Azra & Sunil Bhatia | Holly Carrythers | Maria Daniels | Susan B Eshelman |
| David Adler | Debbie Bier | C Carter | Dr Hillary Dapan | Betsy Espe |
| Kenneth Agabian | Jan Bird | Greg Carter | Michael Dare | Enrique Espinosa |
| Nancy Agabian | Dana Bisbee | S L Casey | Robin Dated | Bachi Esquivel |
| John Agrelius | Ed & Becky Black | Ethan Casson | Cathie Daugherty | Andrew Evans |
| Dana Ahfeldt | Hal Blackwelder | Aldo Castaneda | Michael Davenport | Ed Evansen |
| Tarja Ahlgren | Joan Blaedel Ross | Bill Casti | Nina Davenport | Laura Every |
| Ellen Aho | Betty Blake | Ann Catrin | Jeremy Davidson | L Fairloth |
| Rick Alber | William Blakney | Scott Catto | Lori Davidson | Rob Falk |
| Elizabeth Allbritton | Marlene Blanshay | Clinton Cavanaugh | Steve Davis | Oliver Fallon |
| Ericka & Mike Alexandra | Annie Blevins | David Cerul | Susan & Ken Dawson | Richard Farr |
| Melody Lloyd Allen | Tim Bliss | M Chaisson | Geoffrey Day | Maureen Farrell |
| William Allen | Ethan Bodin | Giles Chaple | Sandra Deal | Peter Farsons |
| Tim Allik | Maria Bogdanovich | Alison Chapman | Sally Dean | Martha Fay |
| Kristan Altamus | James Bogken | Eric Chappell | Patricia Deardorff | Jennifer Febbo |
| Ann Alter | Pamela Boord | Sandi Charton | Fares Deban | Jim & Joan Fee |
| Scott Andersen | Chris Borden | Julianne Chatelain | Philip Deely | P A Feher |
| Liz Anderson | Leslie & Frank Bordonaro | Camilla Chaves | Dennis Defoe | A Felleeyrini |
| Mark Anderson | Vegard Borgen | Ira Chavis | Richard Degeorge | A P Fernandez |
| Terry Anderson | Mrs Roger Boughie | Colin Cheer | Ed DeJesus | Meredith Ferraro |
| Tim Anderson | I Boulanger | Patrick Chekal | Tom Dekay | Yves Fezzani |
| William Anderson | Pat Bourque | Sidney Cherenfant | Jim Delameter | Noah Fickler |
| Sharon Andrews | Jon & Susie Bowers | Arni Chertham | Jeremy Delaney | Ishmael the Fiddler |
| Pip Antonellis | Andrew Boyd | Rebel Chiaradia | Jerry Delaney | Carolyn Fidelman |
| Jeff Appelstein | Toby Boyd | Ganya Chiranakhon | Joe, Jennifer Delaney | David Field |
| Adna Arch | Jason Brabazon | Alexander Chisholm | Tim Delaney | Ken Field |
| Marlene Archer | B Brady | Natt Chomsky | Lisa DeLeon | Alison Fields |
| Kathy Arnold | Susan Brady | Joseph Chonacky | Peggy Dellas | John Filip |
| David Arnold | Andrea Brajuka | Elizabeth Clark | Ermes DeMaria | Maggie Fiman |
| Fred Arnott | Carol Branton | S F Clayton | Melissa DeMarsh | Joseph Finley |
| Judy Ash | Katy Bratun | Mary Clements | M L Demers | Jason Fischer |
| Also Aswell | Jack Braudis | Ellen Clinton | Paul Den | Lynn Fischer |
| Demitrios Athens | Eve Brauner | John Coan | Elissa Denehey | Robert Fischer |
| Nancy Avinger | Greg Braxton | Catherine Cobb | Matthew Dennehy | Opal & Grant Fisher |
| J T Babok | Jerry Brazil | Amil Cockrum | Maryjane Denns | B Fishman |
| Tom Baccei | Christine Bredfieldt | Howard Cohen | Frank der Sarkisian | Renee Fishman |
| Paul Bagley | Karen Bredfeldt | Peter Cohen | Ken DeRonin | Jonathan Fiske |
| Ben Bailey | Marilyn Bregoli | Zoe Cohen | Karen DeRouin | David Fitzgerald |
| Susan Bainbridge | M Brent | Tom & Chris Colamaria | Lionel Dersot | Greg Fitzgerald |
| Ian Baker | Lorraine Brevig | Claudia Colan | Kathryn DeSisto | Jaye Fitzgerald |
| Robert Baker | Fred & Elise Brink | Mark Colan | Ron Deutsch | Neil Fitzpatrick |
| Steven Bakondi | Erik Brisson | Mark Coleman | Damien Devasto | Sean Fitzpatrick |
| Bob Balaban | K Brobeck | Susanne Coleman | Tara Deveaux | Brian Flaherty |
| John & Debbie Baldwin | S J F Brocaar | Barbara Colleton | Lavinia DeVillier | Rosemary Flannery |
| Stephen Baldwin | Harvey Brock | Colette Collin | David Devine | The Flays |
| Mike Ball | Norman Brodesser | Corrie Collin | Margery Dews | Anne Fleisher |
| Michael Balog | Mary Brodie | Pamela Collin | Taney Dich | Dan Fleming |
| Sandy Banghart | William Brokamp | Alan Collins | Jeff Diego | Ellen Fleming |
| Aaron Barcelo | Sondra Brooks | Eric Collins | Mark Dighton | Lynne Flodin |
| Chris Baril | Hilary Bromberg | Judy Collins | Julie Dimatteo | Gary Flood |
| Derren Barken | Barbara Brown | Kevin Collins | Ron Dimon | John Flowers |
| Michael Barker | Chris R Brown | Leo Collins | Charles Dinerstein | Sabina Forbes |
| Tim Barnaby | David Brown | Patrick Collins | David Dirks | Ric Ford |
| Albert Barnes | Howard Brown | Tim Collins | Andy Diskes | Lynelle Forrest |
| Matt & Jane Baronas | Tim Brown | Lisa Colt | Kathleen do Conto | Henry Forster |
| Sheldon Barr | Judith Browne | Joe Comeau | W R Doak | Gretchen Fox |
| Beverly Barrell | Barbara Brownell | Clint Conley | Rick Dochterman | Jon Fox |
| Judy & Barrett John | Jacqueline Bruner | Tom Conneely | Dan Doherty | Michael Frank |
| Dave Barry | D Buckler | Steve Connelly | Edward Doherty | Jackie Frant |
| Glenys Barry | Laura Ann "Boop" Buckles | Mary Connolly | M Doherty | Kara Fraser |
| Scott Bartels | Jan Buckwalter | Rebecca Connolly | Xtorph Dohrman | Mary and Don Fraser |
| Lacey Bartich | Jennifer Budai | Bill Contente | Gerald Donahue | Mark Frauenfelder |
| Dean Barthuly | Matthew Burfiend | John Conway | Henry Donahue | Gerry Fredette |
| William Barkowicz | Tracey & Bill Burg | L Cook | Bonnie Donohue | Jonathan Freedman |
| Scott Bartles | Susan & Dick Burke | Al Cooper | Steve Douglas | Linda Freeley |
| Harriet Baskas | Denis Burkhardt | Linda Corbett | Tony Doyle | Jeremy Freeman |
| Ruth & Jim Bauer | Megan Burling | Brian Corey | Elizabeth Driehaus | Wayne Freno |
| Dasa Bause | Bucks Burnett | Bill Cormier | David Driscoll | Daniel Frey |
| Lana Baziuk | C Burnett | Aileen, Brad Cormiere | Eileen Driscoll | Chad Frost |
| Diane Beach | Misha Burnett | Nicholas Cormiere | Margaret Driscoll | Diana Fry |
| Peter Beamish | Amy Burrer | Brian Corr | Estelle Drozen | Burr Frye |
| Mimi Bean | Maura Butler | Ron Corral | Kathi Drummy | Paul Funk |
| Trevelyn Beard | Lisa Buttiglieri | John Corso | Gary Dryfoos | Charles Furbush |
| Helen Beattie | Wendy Button | Laura Cote | Fran Dublin | Steve Gabany |
| Tom Bechard | Melissa Buxton | Geraldine Coughlin | Rich Ducott | Ray Gagnon |
| Stephanie Becker | Pam Bybell | Joseph Coughlin | Laura Dunbar | Bill Gallagher |
| Martha Bednarz | Kimberlie Rose Byington | Ed Council | Robert Dunbar | Connell Gallagher |
| Beth Beighre | Christopher & Brooke Cabot | P Cox | Denise Duncan | David Gamble |
| Steven Belknap | Denise Caceres | Sally Button Cragin | Sharyn & Tim Duncan | Joseph Garcia |
| Cathleen Bell | Kathy Cahill | Dough Crater | Dennis Dunn | Rich Gardner |
| Jessica Bell | Emory Cain | Terry Creasy | Myrel Dyson III | Matthew Garelick |
| Megara Bell | David Caldwell | Gary Cree | Peggy Earle | Kathy Jones Garmil |
| Nancy Bell | Michael Caligiuri | Caroline Crescenzi | Stella Easland | Laurence Gartel |
| Diana Bella | Elizabeth Call | Mark Cresswell | Marcia Eastabrook | Jeff & Denise Gates |
| Bello Family | Natalie Camelo | Ann & Gerry Cronin | Charles Eaton | Herb Gatti |
| Adam Bellusi | Chester Campbell | Katy Cronin | Eric Eckman | Gina Geary |
| Blair & Nancy Belsito | Duane Campbell | L J Crowley | T A Edison | Andy Gelbert |
| Breudau Bengantuno | Isabella Campbell | Louis Cruz | I Edmonson | Judy Gelman |
| Jamie Bennett | Michael Campbell | Cathy Cullis | Phil Edwards | Raymon Genaro |
| Meg Bennett | Laura Canis | Ellen Cunniff | Fran Egan | Steve Gerow |
| Henry Bennett | Liz Canner | Tom Cunningham | Sterling Eggleston | Michael Gidwitz |
| Julie Benson | Jean Canty | Candace Currie | Eric Elfman | Adonica Gieger |
| Eileen Berg | Vincent Capiello | Patrick Currier | George Ellenbugen | Michael Gierl |
| Glen Berger | Edith Carey | Mr Curt | Heather Ellis | David Gilbert |
| Ronald Berger | Steve Carey | Hal Curtis | Hench Ellis | Ed Gilbert |
| Beth Berghline | Heather Carito | Mark D'Antonio | Richard Tryzno Ellsberry | Frank Gilchrist |
| Walter Bergler | Cob Carlson | John Daily | Steven Ellwanger | Kate Gilmore |

Shaun Gilroy
Sue Gilzow
Barbara Gingrande
Maureen Giorgio
Ellen Gitelman
Richard Gleaves
Jeff Glickman
Todd Glovka
Philip Glynn
Kathleen Godfrey
Judy Godino
John Goessmann
Ellen Goetz
Jane Goguen
Dan Gold
Vickie Gold
Emily Goldberg
Mark Goldfield
Dan Goldgeier
Joe Goldkamp
Dan Goldman
Pat Gomez
Jane Goodrich
Larry Gordon
Greg Gottlieb
Keith Gould
Daniel C Grabonbon
Laurie Graham
David Grahm
Cindy Grant
L M Grant
Taylor Grant
Ellen Welch Granta
Felicity Green
Shelley Green
Jonathan Greenburg
Laurel Greenburg
James Greene
Jodi & Joshua Greenspan
Mark Gregorek
Gabriela Greif
J C Griefeld
Sam Griesmer
Larry Groebe
John Grossmann
Dvid K Gruber
Bob Gruby
Dotty Guild
Ken Guillaume
Sonia Gurevitz
Ray Haack
Carl Haap
John Haas
Kathryn Hackman
Katherine Hadfield
Julie Hafer
Kathleen Hagan
M V Hahn
Eric Haines
Jay Halfond
Douglas Hall
Phil Halfman
Ollie Hallowell
Kimberly Hally-Coleman
Jane Halpert
Stephenie Halpert
Kaitlyn Halpin
Fred & Paige Halsall
Robert Hamlin
David Hanbury
William Hanff
Joe Hannen
Beth Hansen
Gail Hansen
Yannis Haritos
Beth Harrington
Tim Harrington Jr
Jessica Harris
Stacey Harris
Louise Harshburg
Stephen Hart
Perri Hart
Carol Hartman
Sally Hartshorne
Mark Hartwell
Bob Harvey
Brent Hartwerth
Nancy Jo Haselbachen
Greg Hawkins
Ronald Hawkins
Dean Hawthorne
Christine Hayes
Suzanne Hegland
Martha Heid
Charles Heiman
Glenn Helfand
M T Helmes
R C Hemlin
Diane Hendrix
Kristin Henshaw
Tony Hensley
Richard Heoll
Vinie Herbert
Hercules Press

Robin Herman
Christopher Herot
Jim Herron
Adam Hewes
Colby Hewitt
Sean Hewitt
Cynthia Hill
Gregory Hill
Heather Hill
J Hill
Christine Hinkle
Jim Hirsch
Allan Hjerpe
Billie Hockett
John Hodge
Els Hoek
Amy Hoffman
Anne Hoffman
Boris & Ina Hoffman
Maureen Hoffman
Susan Hoffman
Brian Holden
Rebecca Holman
CDR Wayne Horn
Brandon Hoskins
Eric Houston
Jim Howard
Susan Howard
David Howe
Rich Howley
Mary Lou Hubbell
Erica Hruby
Fritz Huber
David Hubner
Michael Hubner
Barbara Hudson
Doug Hughes
Randy Hudson
Erika Huhtamo
Aiden Hume
Alex Humez
Bebe Humphries
Gary Hunnicut
Fraser Hunt
James Hunt
Cherry Hunter
Scott Hunter
Sam Hunting
Nance Hurt
James Hutchins
George Ibarra
Noor Idris
Sofi & Raviv Inbav
Dr & Mrs Leonard Indiana
Gillian Ingham
B Iordachescu
Sarah Irani
David Ireland
Peter Ireland
Randy Isaacson
David Iwatsuki
Dave Jack
Bob Jackson
Carmel Jackson
Daniel Jackson
Debby Jackson
Denis Jackson Jr
Ronald R Jackson
Bill Jacky
Tom Jacky
Richard Jacobs
J Michael James
Nikica Jankovic
Betty Jaros
Lorene Jean
R S Jellinik
Tim Jennett
Diane Jensen
Cynthia Joblin
Glenn Johanson
Betsy, Katie, Susan Johnson
Howard Johnson
Jennifer Johnson
Jane Jolkovski
Bob Jones
David Jones
Dina Jones
Stephen Jones
Taylor Jones
Wayne Jope
Kelly Joyce
Richard Joyce
Bob Judd
C Juhasz
Dave Juppenlatuz
Donald Jurkoic
Dr J & Pat Jurkoic
Jay Jurkoic
Kristin Jurkoic
John Jurkoic
Craig Jurkoic
Chris Justice
Greg Kadel
Jim Koemmerlen

Joel Kahn
Lurey Kahn
Markus Kajo
Ivor Kaklins
Marie Kalat
Katie Lilien Kamp
Joe Kamp
Leah Kane
Robert Kantor
Paul, Sheila, Julie Karian
Tony Karp
Heikki Kastemaa
Jared Katsiane
Melissa Katz
Jill Kaufman
Cathal Kavanagh
Abe Kazuhiro
Laura Keally
Terry Keane
Jeanne Kent
Pamela Keegan
Joyce Keenan
Maureen Keiller
James Keisser
Fab & Roger Keller
Carol Kelley
Diane Kelley
M & D Kelliher
Gail Kelly
John Kelly
Kevin Kelly
Mary Kelly
J M Kennedy
Harry Kenny
Jeanne Kent
L J Kenyon
Kakuna Kerina
Bill & Kathy Kerr
Adelaide Key
Robert Khoerk
George Kimball
Bev & Russ Kimball
Chris King
Michael Kirschenbarm
Bob Klein
Jennifer Kliese
Robert Knoerk
Jim Knowles
David & Rachel Knowlton
David Koepke
Dennis Kois
Ron Kolotnow
June Komisar
Alison Koster
Gary Kostera
Milan Kostic
J M Kraft
Carla Krash
Wolfgang Kraus
Kevin Kraynick
Stig Ronald Krismansen
Lauren Krug
Jan Kubasiewicz
Gert & Jan Kuiper
Prof James Kuiper
Joyce Kulhawik
E J Kuta
Lyda Kuth
Elizabeth Labedz
Richard Lahart
Jason Laird
Randy Lakeman
Laura Lakeway
Donna LaMadeline
Matthew LaMantia
Nine Lambiase
Donald Landmessen
Paulette Landmessen
Maureen Lane
Lois Lane
Valerie Languet
M Lapiann
Susan LaPierre
Mark Vincent Lapolla
Zini Lardieri
E Scott Laughlin
Susan Lawlor
Wendy Lawton
Aimee LeBec
Cathy Lederer
Barry Lederman
Bernard Lee
Randall Lee
Theresa Lee
Robert Leedy
Josh Lehman
Thomas Lehr
Bill Leigh
Krist Leinert
Keith Lemery
Sandy Leonard
Michael Lepera
Lisa Lesniak
Jean LeVangie

Steve Levering
F H Levine
Kathy Sue Levine
Ruth Levitsky
Kathy Lewi
Bob Lewis
Charles Lewis
David & Maura Lewis
Michael Lewis
Peter Lewis
Laura Liebster
Deborah Light
Alexandra Lin
Shih-Ying Lin
Diana Linden
Susan Lindsay
Robert Linehart
Joan Linskey
Joanna Liss
Robert Liston
Josh Livingston
Mary Anne Lloyd
J Locke
Andrew Lockhart
Harry Lohr
Bill Loman
Bobby Long
Chase Long
John Long
Keith Lopes
Patricio Lopez
Robert Lori
Roger Los
Frank Love
Karen Love
Frank Love
Jonathan Lovell
Stacy Lowe
Miles Ludwig
Murray Lufglass
Marco Luschnat
Julie Lutts
Marty Lynch
Andrew Lynn
Keith Lyon
Royal Lyon
John MacDonald
Lee MacDonald
Stacy MacDonald
M MacDonald
Linda Mackey
Michael Macrides
Adam Magazine
Lorraine Magrath
Eric Maheu
Kevin & Polly Mahoney
Douglas Mahr
Greg Mailloux
Martin Maisonjsierre
Virginia Mak
Steve Makris
Marvin Malasky
Judee Malis
Dan Mallach
Efrem Mallach
John Malloy
Rita Maloney
Fiona Manchand
Don Manco
Dona Manfred
Laurel Marcus
Freya M Margand
Dan Margrita
C J Margulis
J Marino
James Marino
Thomas Markle
Fran Markus
Frank Markus
Laura Mars
Susan Marsland
Robert Marsters
Cherie Martin
Joyce Martin
Paul Martin
Joseph & Jami Masalsky
Guillermo Marine Maside
Rene Massey
Frank & Norma Mathy
Paul Matthews
R M Mattola
Derilse Matulis
Jennifer Maxwell
David Maxcy
Sherrie Mayer
Amy Mayer
Jen McCann
Denise McCartin
Melissa McCarthy
Steve McCauley
Dan McCormack
Dan McCrossan
K McCrossan
Claudia McCue

Caleb McCusker
Neil Patrick McDermot
Tracy McDermott
John McDonald
B McDonough
Ed McDonough
Jack & Kelly McDonough
Mary Ellen McDonough
A M McEnery
P D McGinley
S McGinn
Robert McGlinchey
D McGreevey
James McGurl
Ronald McIntire
Ben McIntosh
Doug McIver
Dina Jones McKelly
Thomas McKinley
Matthew McLaughlin
Bridget McManus
D McMillin
John McMurtrie
Linda McNevin
Cathi McParland
Sandra McPherson
Karen DeLorenzo McPhillips
Tim McZoy
Glenn Meader
Mark & Kate Medlar
Tom Meek
Paul Melchin
John Mella
Rich Mella
Richard & Leslie Mella
F Mercadoallene
Janice Merelles
Peter Metlicka
Deborah Sue Metzel
Jennifer Meyer
John Meyers
Elliott R Mibaum
Cindy Micciche
Myran Michaelis
Greg Michetti
Patrick Miehe
Karen Mielcarz
Mimi Miga
A J Miller
Mr E C Miller
Frances Miller
Jodi Miller
L Miller
M J Miller
Michael Miller
Myron Miller
Peter & Marcia Miller
Sara Miller
Scott Miller
Tom Miller
Valerie Miller
Gary & Eilish Mills
Phil Milstein
Laurie & David Mindlin
Kate Mink
Doug Mink
Dympna Minnock
Dan Miranda
Ann & Jack Mitchell
John Mitchell
Lisa Mitchell
Marion Mitchell
Lisa Modecker
Martin Moebus
Ralph Moellers
Jim Mollenauer
Joe Mollery
Pamela Molochko
Leonard Monahan
Sioux Mont
David & Natalie Monteforte
Joseph Montgomery
Troy H Moon
Chip Moore
Dan Moore
Earlene Moore
Ken Moore
Rod Morgan
Eric Morin
Randy Morin
Lucy Morris
Julie Morrison
Frank Morrow
R M Mottola
Patricia Moulick
Aahm Mrafe
Janice Mueller
Kathi Mulhall
John Mullaney
Maria Muller
L N Mullman
C Basilici Murphy
D Murphy
Matthew Murphy

| | | | | | |
|---|---|---|---|---|---|
| Maura Murphy | Lisa Perkins | Tim Robertson | Sheila Selby | Kurt Sussman | Peter Wallace |
| W Murphy | Janet Perlman | Ken Robinson | Sarah Selzer | Gary Susswein | John Walliser |
| Elizabeth Murray | Alma Perry | Lauren Robinson | Leslie Semonian | Takeshi Suzuki | C Walsh |
| Ken Murray | E Perry | T Robinson | Ign Senoadji | Brent Sverdloff | Melissa Walther |
| Susan Murray | Lynn Perry | Walter Robinson | Heath Serfert | John Swanson | Ted Warnell |
| Judi Muscara | Vicky Peters | Dr William Robinson | Reza Shahidi | Robert Sweda | Karen Warner |
| David & Norma Mutch | John Petrexro | Linda Robrish | Tom Shaker | Bill Swislow | Brian Warren |
| Jo-Anne Myers | Bill Phillips | Jan & Alan Robson | Liam Shannon | Kate Switalski | Susan Waterman |
| Lynn Nafey | Carl Phillips | Susie Robson | Joann Shauck | Karlyl Sylken | Sue Waters |
| Scott Nash | Richard Phillips | Eileen Roche | Ivan Shaw | Robert Szuszkiewica | Rachel Watson |
| Charlotte Neagle | Stewart Phillips | Margaret Roche | Zane Sheaffer | Camille Szychalska | John Watt |
| Dr James Neller | Nigel & Julie Pickard | A Rodgers | Jack Sheehan | Jennifer Tachera | Scott Wayne |
| Karen Nelson | R I Pienaar | Cherilyn Roest | James Sheehan | Kristin Taghon | Abigal Weun |
| Matt Ness | Eric Pierce | Jeff Rogers | Craig Sheely | Louise Talbourdet | David Wean |
| Linda M Nevin | Karen Pierce | Jane Rokita | Ken Sheldon | Ed Tallent | J Webb |
| Rob Newberry | Ann Pierson | Katy Rola | Jennifer Shepherd | Florence Tamburro | Michael Weber |
| Dave Newbold | Eleanor Pietrini | Craig Roland | Colin Sheridan | Rebecca Tasker | Leigh Weesner |
| John Newcomer | Barry Mackeral Pike | Gary Roma | Norman Sherwood | Brendy Taylor | Pat Wehrman |
| Christine Newman | Patricia Pink | William Rompala | Jennifer Shiao | Colin Taylor | Deborah Weinstein |
| Daniel J Newquist | Dawn Piso | Justin Rood | Timothy Paul Shields | Elizabeth Taylor | Paul Weinstein |
| Javio Nia | Tony Plamonden | Dan Rose | Victor Shing | Jim Taylor | Alfred Weisberg |
| Lina Nichal | Herve Pledel | Diane Rose | Kevin Shone | Kelly Taylor | David Weisman |
| Pat Nichol | Tyler Polhemus | Mark Rose | Todd Shottock | Ruth Taylor | Bart Weiss |
| K Guild Nichols | Ark Polk | Matthew Rose | Shondra Shumpert | Sidony Taylor | Louis Weiss |
| Max Niedzwiecki | Beulah Polley | Chuck & Miriam Rosenblatt | Dan Sierak | Steve Taylor | Sharon Weiss |
| Henry Nigro | Mark Polonski | The Rosenspans | Asa Simmons | Ty Tempel | F Weissenborn |
| Dean Nimmer | Paul Pomerleau | J S Ross | Jonathan Simon | Mauritis Ternhoven | Anne Welch |
| Kathy Nitchie | Marie Poolicheti | Rich Brisket Roth | Sanjay Singh | Steve Terp | Duncan Welch |
| Tim Nitloff | Zandy Popps | Joan Rothman | Glenn Sinsigalie | A Tetewesky | Matthew Welch |
| Dave Nolan | Michael Porter | Dan Roumagoux | Gregory K Skraznas | Michele Tetreault | Barry Welden |
| Tim Nolan | Henk Portier | Peter Rowe | Nancy & Ron Slate | Ken Textores | Thomas Wellems |
| Derek Nolin | Herman Postma | Anita Rowland | S Slater | Darius Thabit | Charlie Wellock |
| S Nonack | Alicia Potter | Anita Rozsa | Jack Slaughter | Bill Thompson | Rich Wells |
| Img Norman | Greta Poulsen | Philip Rubin | Lois Slavin | Chuck Thompson | Eve Wergley |
| Paul Novacek | Chris Powell | G Albert Ruesga | J D Sloan | Jane Thompson | Marlin Werner |
| Mary & Jerry Novak | Hogsy Power | Glauco Ruesga | Adam Slynotzky | Judy Thompson | Marty Werner |
| Barbara O'Brien | Adrienne Prairie | Brendon Rush | Millen Smail | Mary Lou Thomson | Rob Werner |
| Beth O'Connell | Barbara Prairie | Carol Russell | Sarah Smiley | Tricia Thomson | Roy Wessel |
| John O'Connell | Sesha Pratap | Jacob Hale Russell | Angela Smith | Ivana Tinkle | Dan Wexler |
| Martha & Theresa O'Connell | Allen Pratt | Ray Rustrian | Charlotte Smith | Masahiko Todoroki | William Wharton |
| Stephen & Christine O'Connell | Neil Prentiss | Deirdre & Brenda Ruth | Cheri Smith | Lawrence Tomlin | Dixie Whatley |
| Eileen O'Dea | George Preston | Thomas Ryan | Chris Smith | Fred Tompkins | Becky Whidden |
| Craig O'Donnell | Tony Prince | Joe Sabatini | Joanmarie Smith | R R Topliyn | David Whisnant |
| James O'Donnell | Christine Pritchard | Mandy Sabine | Lani Smith | Michael Travaglini | Carol White |
| Brendan O'Hara | Suzy & Dave Prodanas | Ed Sacco | Owen Smith | Fred & Janice Travers | Harg White |
| Brian O'Hara | Steve Proveyeur | Jeremy Sacco | Steven Smith | Scott Traylor | James White |
| Honor O'Hara | Alan & Beth Pullman | Adam Sacks | Virginia Smith | Cheryl Tree | Suzanne White |
| Joe O'Hara | Hava & Michal Pullman | Ray Saenz | C Snow | Wei & John Tremble | Harvey Wigder |
| Mary O'Hara | Lisa Quaglinto | Ilam Saftoiu | Ray Snyder | Lindsay Trementozzi | William Wilder |
| Mike O'Hara | Richard Quan | Stuart Saginor | Bosco So | John Trenkle | Frances Willenberg |
| Dan O'Neil | Sheridan Quigley | Steve Saleh | Bob Soron | Beth Tresslar | J P Willging |
| William O'Neill | Jon Quillars | Michael Salzman | Noah Southall | Rig Trimby | Becky Williams |
| Carmel & Peter O'Reilly | Anita Quinn | Gary Samett | Steve,& Sue Sowle | Peta Triplett | Bob Williams |
| Brigid O'Riordan | Marilyn Quinn | Janet Sammons | Andrew Sowle | Deborah Trombley | Dina Ann Williams |
| Greg Ofanos | Tom Quinn | Salim Samuel | Cheryl Spahn | Dana Tructman | Ifor Williams |
| Michael Okwu | James Quirk | Maurie Samuels | Craig Spalter | Trzebiatowski Mike | Jeffrey Williams |
| Frank Oldfield | Catherine Racette | Jay Sand | Dave Sparks | Bruce Tsiknas | Thomas Williams |
| Dave Olsen | Julie Rackliffe | Michael Sand | Richard Spector | Paula Tucci | Julian Willis |
| Dale Olson | Casmiro Rael | Diana Sandeglin | William Speer | Peter Turner | Anna, Jay and Wilson |
| James O'Neill | Lois Rafenski | Kristen Sanders | Jon Spencer | Chris Turpin | Emily Wilson |
| Vsevodod Onyshkevych | Amy Ragus | Diana Sandgren | T Spring | Ivana Twinkle | Katherine Wilson |
| Peter Orio | Idris Rahmaan | Jerry Sandholm | Alex St Onge | James Tyler | Len & Rose Wilson |
| Domenico Orsini | Karen Ransom | Gladys Sandmen | Aischa Staal | Max Tzinman | Nancy Wilson |
| Joel Ortila | Annette Raphel | Mark Sandrof | Jean Stankowicz | Chris & Vickie Udden | Rick & Beth Wilson |
| S Otis | Saurabh Rastogi | Linda Sands | Alec Stansell | Jacob Udel | Timothy Wilson |
| Otis the chichuahua | Idris Ratmaan | Susan Santi | James E Starner | Frank Ullenberg | Carl Winderl |
| Mark Outson | Tom Rausenbach | Natalie Santagate | Cathy Steele | Ellen Ullman | Scott Winick |
| Don Owens | Jen Reade | Jim Santagati | Anne Marie Stein | Robert Ullmann | T J Winick |
| Laura Packer | Lucy Reale | Mark Santamaria | Cooper Stein MacDonald | Sigfried Ulmer | Matthew Winn |
| Wendy Page | John Reavey | Alice Santiago | Barry Stein | E R Ulyate | Stuart Winn |
| Laura Paglione | Maria Reidelbach | Rosemary & Bob Sarcia | Liz Stein | Natty Urquizo | George Winslow |
| Paine Family | Bill, Kay & Paul Reilly | Esteban Sardera | Rob Stein | Dr George Usvary | Sanford Winslow |
| Edward Palder | Eileen Reilly | George Sauer | Richard Steinberg | David Valcovic | Sandra Winter |
| Richard Palmer | Michael & Patty Reilly | Phylis Saunders | Bill Steinmetz | Jeffrey Vale | Theresa Wirfree |
| Carolyn Pampino | Sheila Reilly | Maxwell Saunders | Howard Stenger | Chuck Valenza | Dianne Wiroll |
| Tess Panfil | Susan Riley | Jill Sawdon | Nancy Stetzinger | Nina Valery | Denis Wise |
| Brian Pappas | David Reiner | Marion Sawey | Bill Steven | Steve Vallas | Joyce Wiseman |
| Julia Papps | H Reinhard | Barbara Sawhill | Averill Stevenson | Chris Vanderweidt | Carl Witthoft |
| Joanna Parell | Joel Reisman | Buzz Sawhill | Rich Stevenson | J Vaughan | Howard Wolinsky |
| Jessica Parker | Tim Reiter | Jim Sawhill | Bob Stewart | David Veblen | Frank Woo |
| Stephen Parker | Thom Remington | John Elden Sawhill | Duncan Stewart | Tom Veldran | Eric, Nancy & Jim Wood |
| Steven Parker | C Reynold | Don Sawyer | Andrew Stiles | Rene Vespia | David Woodberry |
| Aidan Parkinson | Valerie Rich | Jane Schafer | Ellen & Bruce Still | Trevor Vichas | L Woolferson |
| Joe Parskey | Peterson Richard | Craig Schaffer | Dick Stivers | Andrea Villa | Logan S Wright |
| Stacy Parson | Raven Richardson | Eric Schaffer | Richard Stohlman | Lisa Vinich | Eli Wylen |
| Louise Pascale | Sue Richman | Susanne Schantz | Peter Stohn | Julie Vlasak | Erik & Paul Wysocan |
| Dr & Dr Patchen | Cory Richter | J T Schavone | Art Stone | James Vleck | Bonnie Yablon |
| Paul Paternoster | Jennifer Richter | Per Schenk | David Stone | Bob Voges | Colleen Yachimski |
| Eric Paul | Betsy Riggs | Liz Scherle | Larry Stone | Sharon Vogh | Mr & Mrs Robert Young |
| Morte Payeti | Kevin Riley | John Schlechter | Steve Stone | Lucia Volk | Eric Youngdale |
| Thomas Peacock | Paul Riley | Lothar Schmidt | Virginia Stouffer | Francis Volpe | Charles Zamorski |
| Rachel Pearl | Sue Riley | Frank Schmittrath | Joan & Mike Strauss | Ooola Von Bullow | Larry Zar |
| Andrew Pearson | Victoria Riley | Thomas Schneider | Lee Strauss | Dane Von Rhee | Gabriel Zarate |
| Jill Pearson | William Riley | Robert Schuldenfrei | C Strawbridge | Richard Von Blucher | Frances & Dino Zaros |
| Derek Pell | Giselle Rim | Jim Schulman | Mike Strawbridge | Karan Wad-Jama | Myra Zarrow |
| Anne Pellagrini | A Ripp | Ford Schumann | Robin Strober | Cathie Walker | Juliana Zee |
| Marianne Pendleton | Robert Rippen | Jonathan Schwanbeck | Chuck Strubbe | Dawn Walker | Jeffrey Zeizel |
| Joseph Pensack | Heath Ritchie | Rob Scudder | Felicia Sullivan | Mike Walker | Richard Zemen |
| Gerard Perez | Billy Rivera | Martha Seeley | Kathleen Sullivan | Duncan Wall | The Zemons |
| Michael Perin-Wogenburg | Ken Roberts | Marti Seely | Meg Sullivan | Brian Wallace | Sherry Zipp |
| S Perino | Mike Roberts | Lisa Seibert | Mike Sullo | Jean Wallace | Stanley Zukowsky |
| Joan Perkins | David Robertson | Courtney Seiler | Lou Susi | Kelly Wallace | |